Through the Mill

To Brian with Best wishes
from Stephen

(December 1987)

IAN BEESLEY

The Story of
Yorkshire Wool in Photographs

Introduction by Gary Firth

Dalesman Books

in association with

National Museum of Photography, Film & Television

1987

The Dalesman Publishing Company Ltd.,
Clapham, Lancaster, LA2 8EB

First published 1987

ISBN: 0 85206 894 8

Front cover by Long & Stebbens Graphic Design

Printed by Fretwell & Cox Ltd.,
Healey Works, Goulbourne Street, Keighley, West Yorkshire BD21 1PZ

Foreword

IN 1984 Ian Beesley came to the National Museum of Photography, Film & Television with a portfolio of photographs. As he showed us his work he described how, some years earlier, he had set himself the task of photographing the wool industry of his native Yorkshire. In his spare time he had photographed numerous mills and other wool industry buildings before they had been demolished. He had also started to photograph some aspects of the industry in more detail; the photographs of Undercliffe Cemetery in this book are from just such a study.

This was undoubtedly an ambitious project. One person working during evenings and weekends could only just keep ahead of the demolisher's bulldozer, let alone record the many side industries and the process of change within the industry itself. What Ian needed were the resources to work full-time for a year on his project. At the Museum we were impressed with his enthusiasm and commitment, as well as by his photographic skills. We felt that the project itself was important, given that wool had played, and continues to play, such an important part in the economy and working life of Yorkshire, and we set about raising the money for the project. We were pleased to find that others felt as we did, and were able to support Ian's work in a variety of ways.

From mid 1985 and throughout most of 1986 Ian was able to carry out his project. This book, and the 1987 exhibition of photographs at the National Museum of Photography, are the product of that work. What you see here is the history of wool in Yorkshire from the Bronze Age, through the period of the monasteries in the Middle Ages, to the age of industrialisation in the nineteenth century, and up to the present. The book also records the processes through which wool passes as it is changed from a raw material into finished cloth, and shows some important side industries such as bobbin and shuttle making.

Photography, it has to be said, has its limitations; there are certain kinds of information that it cannot communicate. For that reason the book starts with an introduction by Gary Firth, an historian who has made a significant contribution to our understanding of the wool industry. This introduction acts as a fine complement to Ian Beesley's evocative and informative photographs.

Terry Morden
Exhibitions Officer
National Museum of Photography, Film & Television

Acknowledgements

We should sincerely like to thank the following for their generous sponsorship which made this project possible:

    Ilford

    The Sam Chippendale Foundation

    Bradford Metropolitan Council's Economic Development Unit, with the Department of the Environment

    West Yorkshire County Council

We are grateful to the following companies and individuals for their help and co-operation:

A & M Textiles, Stanningley
Benson Turner Ltd, Wyke
Brackendale Spinning Co, Thackley
Bradford Conditioning House
Bradford Industrial Museum
British Mohair Spinners Ltd
British Wool Marketing Board
Harry Burnett
Busfield Ltd, Guiseley
Bairstow Cawthra & Co, Halifax
Roger Charnley and Helen Maskill, Confederation of British Wool Textiles Ltd
Colne Valley Museum, Golcar
Crossleys Shuttles, Todmorden
Joseph Dawson Ltd, Bradford
Dixon's Bobbin Mills, Steeton
Mr Ellis, Craghouse Farm
The Fabric Shop, Addingham
George Feather
John Foster & Sons Ltd, Queensbury
Hattersley Ltd, Keighley
Mr D Illingworth, Bracken Hall Farm

Illingworth Morris PLC
International Wool Secretariat
C M Kelly
Leggots Foundry
Lister & Co Ltd, Bradford
Mike Long
Raymond McHugh
Kate Mason
Merchant Adventurers' Hall, York
The National Trust
Pecket Well Mill, Hebden Bridge
Salts of Saltaire
Arthur Saul
Stroud Riley Drummond, Bradford
Geo Strausse, Batley
Wallbank & Parkin Ltd, Bradford
Hilda Watkinson
Weavercraft Carpets Ltd
Sam Weller & Sons Ltd
W & J Whitehead Ltd, Bradford
Woolcombers Ltd, Bradford

Finally, thanks to the National Museum of Photography, Film & Television — especially Terry Morden, Exhibitions Officer, for his support and enthusiasm.

— **Ian Beesley and Gary Firth**
March 1987

Introduction

The Early Wool Industry in Yorkshire

WE'VE made cloth in West Yorkshire from the very earliest times. On the windswept, exposed ridges of the Pennines our Stone Age forefathers doubtless felt the need to use the pelts and skins of the wild goats and sheep to keep out the harsh winds of winter. In time, the beasts were domesticated and their shorn fleeces were worked through the basic processes of spinning and weaving. The manufacture of woollen cloth became a central occupation of Yorkshire folk and, apart from farming, was the main feature of the region's economic life for many centuries. On their simple upright looms the people of Bronze Age Yorkshire, c2000 B.C., wove a rudimentary cloth. Numerous spindle whorls and loom weights from the period have been found by archaeologists throughout the county.

From c1500 B.C. the county was attacked by wave after wave of foreigners and migrants from other lands, and as the men farmed and fought to protect what was theirs, the women continued, generation after generation, to weave and spin and provide coarse textiles of thick woollen cloth. The Angle, Saxon, Viking and Norman all encouraged this manufacture of cloth as they successively settled the vales and dales of Yorkshire, more particularly on the lush grassy terrain of the Yorkshire Wolds where rich and poor alike reared sheep, as crucial to their economy as was the buffalo to the North American Indian.

During the twelfth century several monasteries (**plate 5**), particularly the Cistercian, were given large tracts of land by the feudal Norman lords to provide prayers for them and their families after death. On this land the monks reared large flocks of sheep around the beautiful and isolated abbeys which they built at Fountains, Rievaulx and Jervaulx. Wool became the chief source of income for many of these orders. For example, the Cistercians of Fountains Abbey drove their large flocks from Mastiles Lane (**3**) to be shorn at Kilnsey. From there the wool was taken by pack-horse over Pateley Moor to Fountains. There, the fleeces were stored in the Cellarium (**6**) of the abbey awaiting the arrival of merchants from Lombardy and Flanders. Curiously, much of the English wool produced at this time was not woven at home but exported for manufacture by the skilled weavers of Belgium and Northern Italy. In order to pay for their extravagant building programmes, several monastic houses sold wool under forward contracts, mortgaging property and spending money long before the wool had even grown on the sheep's back. Needless to say most of them got into debt. Fountains Abbey, for example, was £6,373 in arrears in 1275 and went cap in hand to the Jews of York. At one time the monks of Fountains devoted 600,000 acres of land to the production of wool, bringing in the fleeces from granges all over northern England, a principal one being at Kilnsey.

At this time the exportation of raw wool was as important to the monarchs of England as it was to the merchants of York or the abbots of Rievaulx and Fountains. This importance is epitomised by the Woolsack in the House of Lords at Westminster. This is the official seat of the Lord Chancellor, the most important of the medieval kings' administrators. The Woolsack demonstrates the importance of the wool trade as a source of revenue to kings of the Middle Ages.

Although much of the Yorkshire 'clip' was exported abroad at this time, there was a small proportion of the raw wool devoted to the manufacture of cloth by the rural population of Yorkshire. It must be remembered that only during and after the fourteenth century was there a significant increase in the amount of cloth woven in England. However, there was by 1150 a moderately large organisation of weavers at York and, later, at Beverley. Other principal Yorkshire towns also had their weaving fraternities including Whitby and Selby. In fact the industry was widespread across all three Yorkshire ridings. In West Yorkshire there is documentary evidence of cloth making during the twelfth century at Leeds, Wakefield, Calverley and numerous references to fulling mills in the Calder Valley. In the North Riding, at Northallerton, Ripon, Richmond and Pickering, various branches of the industry were carried on. An unsophisticated rural industry occurred also to the south at Sheffield and Pontefract. Yet, the amount and quality of these Yorkshire cloths was so low that very little found its way abroad. Indeed Yorkshire merchants continued to import Continental cloths into the county, via Hull, until well after 1300.

All this changed quite significantly during the fourteenth century, when the export of manufactured woollen cloth came to be a central feature in England's medieval economy. By 1330 there was a thriving manufacture of woollen cloth throughout Yorkshire. This buoyancy was consolidated by a series of statutes passed by Edward III which encouraged the settlement of Flemish immigrant weavers into the county. The Flemish weavers came in great numbers to the city of York, and not surprisingly showed little liking for the rural townships of the West Riding, apart from Peter of Brabant, and his son of the same name, who came to live in Sheep Street, Skipton, as weavers of cloth.

Another major feature of the Yorkshire textile industry in the later thirteenth century was the shift of the centre of production away from the big cities like York and Beverley to the country villages of West Yorkshire where the introduction of the spinning wheel was slow to replace the ancient distaff. Spinning was long held to be an occupation for the women of the house (a single woman is still a spinster and until quite recently the female line of the family was known as the distaff side).

The decline of the textile industry in the larger towns of the county has been attributed to a number of causes, the principal one of which was the continued exclusivity of the urban guilds at places like York and Beverley. The internal organisation of the guilds became vigorously over-regulated with bye-laws, and over-taxed with guild levies. Together these two factors prevented the development of skilled enterprise and in consequence all progress in the textile industries at York and Beverley was held up. However, in the countryside, particularly in the West Riding, the industry was free from such encumbrances and was actually encouraged by lower production costs and an ineffective system of local government. York's demise is described in the corporation minute books as early as June 1561:

'The cause of the decay of the . . . weavers and loomes for woollen cloth within the sayd cite as I doe understand and learn is the lak of cloth makeying in the sayd cite as was in old time accustomed whiche is nowe encreased and used in the townes of Halyfax, Leedes and Wakefield for that not only the comodytie of the water-mylnes is ther nigh at hande but also the poore folke as speynners, carders and other necessary workfolkes for the sayd webbing, may ther besyde ther hand labour, have rye, fyre and other releif goode cheape, which is in this cite very deare and wantying.'

By 1550 York's supremacy of the textile industry was almost at an end, although the craft guilds there struggled to survive beyond the seventeenth century. Although the manufacture of woollen cloth in York went into a decline the city continued to play an important part on the merchanting side of the industry. This was done mainly through the activity of the Merchant Adventurers, an association of Yorkshire merchants evolving from the Company of Mercers. Since 1407 they had held royal recognition and became something of a monopoly of wholesale traders in cloth with similar companies at Hull, Bristol and Newcastle, and a headquarters in Hamburg. It was at the Merchant Adventurers Hall in York **(8)** that the merchants purchased the products of the country clothiers and organised their shipments abroad. The company was not an association of capital, for each member was to carry on his own business and conduct his own affairs, but on their three-masted ships these men exported Yorkshire cloth and brought back corn, silks, wines, oils as well as shipbuilding supplies like timber, hemp and tar. One such 'adventurer' was William Wooller (died 1597), a native of Bingley where the cloth trade was expanding during the Elizabethan period. As there is no record of Wooller's apprenticeship Wooller presumably bought his way into the Merchant Adventurers after a successful career as a clothier in Airedale. He was admitted a Freeman of the City of York in 1587 and six years later was a Chamberlain of that city. He was buried in the south aisle of York Minster and his name stands first on the list of benefactors displayed in the Merchant Venturers Hall at York.**(9)** Wooller, in his will, gave liberal legacies for the erection of a free school in Bingley.

The Tudor period was remarkable for two major new developments in the industry. By the end of the sixteenth century 'fickle' fashion turned her back on traditional woollen cloths and the Mediterranean markets suddenly required a finer, lighter cloth for wear in the warmer climate. The skill to make these 'new draperies' was provided by Dutch emigré weavers, religious refugees who had settled in East Anglia and Kent after 1560. New 'draperies' or stuffs required long-combed wool like that produced since the fourteenth century from around Norwich and known as worsted. The name is derived from the East Anglian village of Worstead which was regarded as the main area of worsted cloth production until usurped by the West Riding of Yorkshire in the second half of the eighteenth century.

The wool for worsted cloth was 'combed' as opposed to 'carded' as in the preparation of woollen cloth. The wool was combed by means of two heavy hand implements, the heads of which contained a hundred or more metal prongs on which the wool was fixed. One comb, containing the wool, was attached to an upright cottage beam whilst the second comb was kept warm on a charcoal-fired comb pot — as in the surviving rural combshop at Addingham Moorside in Wharfedale. **(10)** The wool on the first comb was then combed by the second to remove the short fibres (noils) and to produce slivers of long combed wool (tops). Woolcombing was generally admitted to be the most unhealthy branch of the industry and yet the handcombers were regarded as the aristocrats of labour in the cloth trade. They were a highly organised body of men even in the eighteenth century when certain public houses were for combers only and no one else from the industry dared to step inside. Combed or carded wool was then passed to the domestic spinners, who by the end of the fourteenth century were spinning by means of the single-thread spinning wheel rather than the ancient distaff. The yarn was spun largely by the women and young girls of the family and, occasionally, very young children were employed. However hard they worked, the spinners never seemed to be able to supply enough yarn for the weaving process. Moreover, they were rarely able to bring a consistency to the quality of the yarn they produced. It was often too easily broken or inadequately twisted; also it was difficult for all but the most experienced spinster to make all the yarn with the same twist and thickness.

The weaving process, prior to the introduction of the flying shuttle in 1733, was done on a horizontal loom (13) on which the weft-carrying shuttle was passed from hand to hand through the alternate warp thread. The usual cloth made was a 'Kersey' which was a cheap, narrow cloth of one yard wide and 16–18 yards long. Wider cloths were made on a broadloom which required two men, one at either end of the loom. Weavers were plagued by a shortage of yarn and the frequent breaking of poor quality yarn. Furthermore, it was their responsibility for putting the 'piece' of woven cloth through a series of time-consuming 'finishing' processes. In order to mat the warp and weft together the cloth was treated with a mixture of cow dung and urine and other foul-smelling pigments and trampled on. Woollen cloth was now ready for 'fulling' and taken to the nearest fulling mill to mat it by means of dipping the pieces of cloth in a mixture of water and fullers' earth. A water-powered fulling mill beat the fibres together by large heavy hammers or stocks, although a worsted cloth did not need this 'felting' process and consequently most fulling mills were to be found in those parts of Yorkshire which concentrated on producing woollen cloth. The introduction of the fulling process in the thirteenth century and the proximity of the fulling mills to fast running streams was another reason for the transfer of the industry from the large towns into the West Yorkshire countryside. From the fulling mill the cloth went to be 'tentered' or stretched on a frame by means of tenterhooks (hence the expression 'being on tenterhooks') in the clothier's own yard or garden plot. Sometimes there was a specific location, a tenter ground or tenter-croft (14), in each township where the cloth was stretched and dried. As early as 1354 the Bradford Manor Court Rolls identify the town's chaplain as taking his cloths to the tenter ground to be dried.

Finally, the woollen cloth was brushed with teasels to raise the nap and then sheared or cropped of protruding fibres to leave a smooth but soft and fluffy finish. By this time the cloth was ready to be sold to the foreign or domestic merchant.

These were the major processes of production of the Yorkshire woollen industry for several centuries but by 1600 that industry was dominated by the domestic clothier, often a farmer and his family whose Pennine lands were a handicap and who turned his hand, initially in a small way; to a little weaving and woollen cloth production. In time, the independent domestic clothier came to be a key figure in Yorkshire's economic life. By far the best account of this group was given in the Halifax Act of 1555 where the people of Halifax are described thus:

> 'they do altogether live by clothmaking and the great part of them neither getteth corn nor is able to keep a horse to carry wools, nor yet to buy much wool at once, but hath been ever used to repair to the town . . . to buy some a stone, some two, and some three or four according to their ability, and to carry the same to their houses, some three, four, five and six miles off, upon their heads and backs, and so to make and convert the same either into yarn or cloth, and to sell the same and so buy more wool . . .'

The growth of Halifax from the fifteenth century was quite spectacular. Halifax cloth became famous throughout England and the town's prosperity and industry became matters of wonder and congratulation to visitors and Yorkshire folk alike. Leeds, Wakefield and Bradford also became famous as markets and centres of cloth production. However, the economic progress of these towns was hindered by the Civil War, for all of them as well as the port of Hull were sympathetic to the Parliamentary cause. Leeds and Bradford came under the siege guns of the Royalist forces led by the Duke of Newcastle. Bradfordians centred their defence upon the tower of the parish church which they fortified with sheets and bales of wool from the town's clothiers. Bradford finally capitulated, lives were lost and property destroyed as the Royalist army swarmed ruthlessly through the streets. All trade and business was badly interrupted. No sooner had the war passed them by than the West Riding clothing towns were hit by plague in 1645. Streets were deserted and markets transferred to the countryside. During the plague, woollen cloths and bales of wool were scalded in hot water or put into a running stream for two days and then dried in the open air to prevent the spread of the disease.

In spite of these setbacks the West Yorkshire clothiers continued to provide initial capital; to buy the raw material, to supervise the wool through all the processes and to market the finished piece of cloth, in hopes of better times. The Yorkshire clothier might employ only members of his family but some clothiers operated in a 'bigger way', employing large numbers of spinsters and journeymen weavers to work up the cloth for them in their own homes or occasionally in centralised loomshops like that of John Cockshott of Addingham which housed sixty-two handlooms.(12) Such larger 'master clothiers' tended to characterise the cloth industry of the West Country but in Yorkshire the manufacture was largely dominated by small independent clothiers who, by 1600, were especially concentrated in the Halifax area, a fact noted by the well-travelled Daniel Defoe in 1724:

> 'The sun shining we could see that almost at every house there was a tenter, and almost on every tenter a piece of cloth, or kersie or shalloon, for they are the three articles of that country's labour; from which the sun glancing, and as I may say shining, the white reflecting its rays, to us, I thought it was the most agreeable sight that I ever saw, for the hills . . . rising and falling so thick, and the vallies opening sometimes one way, sometimes another . . . yet look which way we would high to the tops and low to the bottoms it was all the same, innumerable houses and tenters and a white piece upon every tenter.'

This proliferation of independent clothiers, particularly in and around Halifax, marked an important stage in the shift from an agrarian to an industrial economy in West Yorkshire. This has been traditionally explained by the appropriate and numerous supplies of water and coal and also the plentiful supply of wool from Pennine sheep. None of these factors satisfactorily answers the growth and development of the West Yorkshire woollen industry in the seventeenth century. A stronger case for this move from land to industry can be made for changes in tenurial factors. Firstly, the quality of land in the Pennine foothills did not considerably interest absentee landowners, particularly the Crown, and consequently manorial control of land tenure was not as rigorous as it was in areas where the land was more productive and profitable. This left owner-occupiers the freedom to do with the land as they wished, a consequence of which was that partible inheritance replaced primogeniture (inheritance of all the land to the first son). This continuous subdivision of land over several generations diminished the size of estates so that farming alone was unable to provide an adequate income for West Yorkshire farmers. An alternative economy had to be found for this growing and densely settled rural population — this was to be the domestic woollen industry.

Another factor which further facilitated this move from agriculture to industry was the financial ease with which it might be done, by even the smallest farmer. The capital requirements of a clothier were low under the domestic system: his most expensive item was the purchase of the raw wool. Much of our understanding of the activities of the domestic clothier has come from the inventories attached to their wills proved in the Archbishop's courts at York. These records also highlight the more substantial contribution made to Yorkshire's dual economy by that of the yeoman clothiers who were owners of large estates as well as large-scale manufacturers of cloth. The wealth generated by these men in their industrial and agricultural activities is best seen in the appearance of numerous low-gabled buildings of stone which proliferated the valleys of Airedale and Calderdale after 1600 (Butler House, Baildon; Beckfoot, Bingley; Peel House, Gomersal). These houses served both as homes and workplaces, invariably including a workshop.

Peel House, Gomersal

The Yorkshire Worsted Industry

Even before the Civil War, West Yorkshire spinners had turned to the production of worsted, as opposed to woollen, yarn. This yarn went into the manufacture of mixed cloths or 'bocking bays' (woollen weft and worsted warp) which were increasingly exported after 1700. West Yorkshire worsted manufacturers also became famous for their 'shalloon' cloths which were wholly of worsted yarn. This distinct worsted industry had been known in Yorkshire in the fourteenth century but had almost disappeared by the sixteenth century. It reappeared after 1670 and eventually became identified with those townships between the rivers Aire and Calder, principally at Halifax and Bradford. It was probably the larger and wealthier woollen clothiers who pioneered this transition to worsted cloth production during the third quarter of the seventeenth century when the woollen industry was marked by stagnation and recession. The transition was not an easy one; a new and different fabric posed labour and technological problems as well as marketing difficulties at home and abroad. A leading protagonist of the development of the worsted trade was Sam Hill at Soyland, six miles from Halifax. Hill, during the 1730s, despaired of this new branch of the Yorkshire wool textile trade, but eventually it won through as West Yorkshire replaced East Anglia as England's principal producer of worsted cloth thirty years later. This expansion of the worsted branch of Yorkshire wool textiles has been attributed to a small number of master manufacturers with large amounts of capital, who 'put out' their wool at various stages of production to the skilled artisans, the journeyman weavers in their own homes.(13)

In order to understand more clearly this development of the Yorkshire worsted trade at this time, it might be helpful to examine the activities of two individual manufacturers. Firstly, a master manufacturer and merchant of considerable status, John Hustler of Bradford, a prominent and distinguished figure who made important institutional changes to the industry in the late eighteenth century; and secondly Robert Heaton of Stanbury, relatively insignificant, but one of hundreds of small manufacturers whose operations in the trade are typical and, moreover, well documented in a detailed collection of business papers.

John Hustler and the Worsted Committee

John Hustler was the son of William Hustler who had married Jane Jowett of Bolton near Bradford in 1714. Both were Quakers and brought up their son, born in the year following, in that faith. John also followed his father in farming the lands at Apple Tree Farm, Low Fold, Bolton in Bradford. William had also functioned as a wool merchant, or stapler, and John, after completing an apprenticeship as wool sorter in 1740, joined his father as a stapler of wool and distributor of cloths. Some indication of his growing status can be seen in the important but unsuccessful part he played in the marked-wool controversy of 1752. Woollen merchants all over the country clamoured for legislation to control brandings and false windings practised by English sheep farmers and complaining of the high price of their wool. Hustler represented West Yorkshire on a committee which petitioned parliament. He testified on their behalf but to no avail.

A quarter of a century later he had more success with the establishment of a union of merchants and manufcturers, the Worsted Committee. The domestic system was a widespread means of production but was open to wide abuse from the operatives. With the expansion of the labour force, and the rising price of good English wool, the manufacturers were faced with an ever-increasing number of embezzlements and thefts. Combers would extract wool for their own use. Spinners reeled short hanks of yarn and there were direct thefts of cloth pieces. Detecting frauds of this nature proved difficult and bringing them before law proved expensive. Consequently, by 1775 northern worsted merchants and manufacturers demanded a confirmation of the laws and an efficient body to enforce them. There had been some form of manufacturer's union before that time, but it had proved ineffective. The Worsted Acts of 1777 were the result of several petitions and appeals from the northern worsted manufacturers. These Acts prohibited malpractices, which had hitherto gone unpunished, through the founding of the Worsted Committee.

At a meeting at the Talbot Inn, Halifax, 9th June 1777, the new system of inspection and supervision was launched. A Yorkshire committee, consisting of seventeen worsted merchants from the main towns — Halifax (6), Bradford (4) — elected John Hustler as its chairman. Lancashire and Cheshire also had their own committees. These area committees were responsible for the execution of the provisions of the Acts. There was to be a team of seven area inspectors whose full-time job it was to investigate and bring to court any transgressors of the statutes. At the third meeting of the Worsted Committee at the Crown and Cushion Inn, Bradford, William Haley of Horton was appointed Superintendent of the inspectorate. John Hustler's industry and enterprise were acknowledged in January 1778 when the committee offically thanked him for his services.

The Worsted Committee certainly proved an effective remedy against fraudulent practice. Inspector Thomas Hardcastle was active in prosecuting the embezzling woolcombers of Bradford and Horton. However, this was not the only function of the Committee, for it encouraged new inventions, suppressed unions and encouraged the trade generally.

Another major crisis to affect both the Yorkshire worsted and woollen trades occurred in the early 1780s. Hustler and the Worsted Committee were once again at the very heart of the new controversy. The agricultural improvements in sheep breeding and increased enclosure for pastures produced a temporarily overstocked domestic market for wool after 1780. The woolgrowers of Lincolnshire and Kent were prevented by law from seeking higher prices abroad and exporting English wool but in December 1781 they sought to repeal such prohibitive statutes. The northern Worsted Committee reacted immediately by appointing Messrs. Hustler, Currer, Clapham and Hebdin to attend a meeting at Lincoln and give their point of view against the exportation of wool. A parliamentary commission of January 1782 (before which Hustler testified) turned down the request of the woolgrowers to export English wool. Nevertheless, in East Anglia and along the Yorkshire Coast, particularly at Robin Hood's Bay, illegal exportation occurred on a very large scale. Hustler was able to offer a solution, for he had 'had the satisfaction of being the planner . . . and being Chairman and Treasurer from 1764 to 1776, of a committee at the small expense of less than £600'. Apparently, before the creation of the Worsted Committee, Hustler had led and operated a combination of manufacturers. Part of their function had been the prevention of exporting worsted yarn. This was affected through the appointment of ten mounted officers at £250 per annum who would visit places along the coastline and make known the laws and penalties regarding smuggling. Hustler estimated for the parliamentary committee that the annual English wool clip was 600,000 packs (144 million pounds) of which 11,000 found their way out of the country. The outcome of this crisis was that the growers were refused permission to export their wool. As a result, smuggling reached new heights in subsequent years. Finally, in 1787, the situation was so bad that the Worsted Committee petitioned parliament for more stringent control of illegal exportation. The result was a new act in 1788 confirming the illegality of exporting English wool.

Thus, Hustler's committees centralised the interests of the northern worsted manufacturers whose theatre of operations covered a very large area. The Worsted Committee had protected their rights and welfare as a commercial group. At a time when central government influence in the provinces was weak, the Committee acted of its own accord, financed by a drawback of the soap duty, allowed to each manufacturer. It was a central and representative body of an otherwise disorganised number of manufacturers and merchants, functioning under the shapeless and scattered system of domestic production. Hustler had played a large part in its foundation and its subsequent workings. Hustler in the period 1766 to 1782 had provided, for the Yorkshire worsted manufacturers and merchants, an institutional framework within which the progress of the trade was developed and co-ordinated by its numerous entrepreneurs.

Robert Heaton — Master Clothier

One of these entrepreneurs was Robert Heaton of Stanbury, near Haworth, who was born in 1726, the son of a substantial yeoman-farmer. He was typical of the many stuff makers in West Yorkshire in the last quarter of the eighteenth century. His three marriages brought additions to the original family estate at Ponden Mill, Stanbury, as well as three sons and a daughter. After 1750, the hall had fallen into disrepair and Robert Heaton moved to Bridge House, in Haworth. From there, he held all the local offices and for several years was a trustee to Haworth Grammar School. His estates, including Ponden, were mostly leased out, for Heaton made his living by the wool trade and did so from the age of twenty-three.

Heaton worked on the putting-out system, employing two agents, John Irwen (up to 1760) and his successor, Joseph Shackleton, who carried wool and yarns to the outworkers along the packhorse trails of the Pennine countryside. In the 1760s Heaton purchased some of his wool from the well known staplers of Bradford like William Hardcastle and John Hustler. He did not venture to the markets and fairs of Lincolnshire himself. Eric Sigsworth has estimated that Heaton was employing over forty domestic spinners in the 1760s, some living in the vicinity, others farther afield. His agents often travelled well into Lancashire to deliver wool and collect yarn from as far afield as Whalley, Bispham and Thornton Cleveleys. After 1761 Heaton began to work the yarn into worsted shalloons employing his weavers from the immediate vicinity. His account books show that the weavers were usually small tenant farmers occupying Heaton's Haworth lands. These men Heaton took into his employ and paid them wages by redeeming them of their rents. In 1775 John Sugden was

Bridge House, Haworth

> 'paid in spinning and weaving and money — in all, this is for Whitsunday Rents for the year 1774. In received £10.'

In this way Heaton obviated the use of cash wages, for specie was often in short supply. Also, by employing his own tenants he lessened the risk of embezzlement and theft. Heaton was, in effect, a forerunner of the factory owner, employing large numbers of workers, purchasing large amounts of raw material and whose output was considerably greater than the small independent clothiers who tended to dominate the Yorkshire woollen trade. Heaton, like other West Yorkshire manufacturers in the domestic system, sold his finished goods at the Cloth Halls or Piece Halls.

Cloth/Piece Halls

In 1600 fifteen Yorkshire townships were entitled to hold cloth fairs but Leeds was by far and away the most important. There, all manner of cloths were sold from trestle tables on the narrow bridge over the River Aire at the bottom of Briggate. Each Tuesday and Saturday the West Yorkshire clothiers brought in their single pieces of cloth to the open-air trading of the Leeds Cloth Market. Daniel Defoe was much impressed by this busy scene:

> 'about six o'clock in summer and seven in winter, the clothiers all being come by that time, the market bell at the old chapel by the bridge rings, upon which it would surprise a stranger to see in how few minutes, without hurry, noise, or the least disorder, the whole market is filled, and all the boards . . . covered with cloth, as close as the pieces can lie longways, each proprietor standing behind his own piece, who form a mercantile regiment as it were, drawn up in a double line in as great order as a military one. As soon as the bell has ceased ringing, the factors and buyers enter the market, and walk up and down between the rows as occasion directs. Some of them have their foreign letters or orders, with patterns sealed on them, in their hands, the colours of which they match by holding them to the cloths they think they agree to. When they have fixed upon their cloth, they lean over to the clothier, and by a whisper in the fewest words

imaginable the price is stated. One asks and the other bids; they agree or disagree in a moment. The reason for this prudent silence is owing to the clothiers standing so near to one another, for it is not reasonable that one trader should know another's traffick. If a merchant has bidden a clothier a price, and he will not take it, he may follow him to his house, and tell him that he has considered it, and is willing to let him have it. But they are not to make any new agreement for it, so as to remove the market from the street to the merchant's house. In a little less than an hour all the business is done, in less than half an hour you will perceive the cloth begin to move off, the clothier taking it upon his shoulder to remove it to the merchant's house. About 8.30 o'clock the market bell rings again, upon which the buyers immediately disappear. The cloth is all sold, or if any remains, it is generally carried back to the inn. By nine the boards and trestles are removed, and the streets are left at liberty for the market people of other professions, line drapers, shoemakers, hardwaremen, sellers of wood vessels, wicker baskets, etc. . . . Thus you see 10 or 20,000 pounds' worth of cloth, and some times much more bought and sold in little more than an hour, the laws of the market being the most strictly observed that I ever saw in any market in England.'

White Cloth Hall, Leeds

By 1710 enclosed Cloth Halls elsewhere in the county challenged the supremacy of the Leeds Market and caused the Leeds merchants to bestir themselves and open a fine new hall for White Cloths in Kirkgate in 1711. In 1755 a larger White Cloth Hall was opened and a third one was erected in 1775. Manufacturers of coloured woollen cloth opened a separate hall for their goods in 1756 and Leeds also housed a Mixed Cloth Hall.

These Leeds Cloth Halls were not the only ones in Yorkshire nor were they even the first in the county. A single-storey building was erected about 1550 at Heptonstall and named Blackwell Hall after the famous cloth market in London. By 1700 it had been converted into cottages as Heptonstall was outpaced by Halifax where the huge and magnificent 315-room Piece Hall (15) was opened in 1779 for the sale of both woollen and worsted cloths. Six years earlier Bradford manufacturers had subscribed towards the building of a Piece Hall in Bradford, specifically for worsted cloth. There were other Cloth Halls at Wakefield (1710), Huddersfield (1766) and Colne. Such was the method of marketing finished cloth before 1800. From the handlooms of scattered cottages came hundreds of unfinished individual pieces of cloth to be purchased by all manner of merchants from the small tailor/shopkeeper to the large foreign merchant trading with Europe and North America. These merchants commissioned croppers, dressers and dyers to finish the pieces or directly employed such men to work on them.

Worsted clothiers like Robert Heaton were also swift to spot the commercial advantages of new inventions in textile technology which had been successfully introduced to the Lancashire cotton industry in the 1760s. Hargreaves' 'spinning-jenny' enabled spinning outputs to keep pace with the yarn requirements of the weavers, particularly when these new machines, originally hand-powered, were harnessed to water power.

Water-powered Spinning Mills

Wealthy and ambitious master manufacturers of Yorkshire worsteds soon took on board these technological developments and the first recorded water-powered worsted spinning mill in Yorkshire was opened at Low Mill, Addingham in 1786. Others followed at Wilsden, Oxenhope and Keighley in the last decade of the eighteenth century. (19)

Like the worsted branch of the industry, woollen cloth production borrowed several technological innovations from the Lancashire cotton industry to take it into the factory age. The inventions of Hargreaves and John Kay had been taken up by West Yorkshire woollen clothiers by 1780 but neither disturbed the domestic system of production. Richard Arkwright's carding machine of 1775 led to the introduction of scribbling mills and hand carding gave way to mechanised operations in water-powered, and later, steam-powered factories. But the transition to factory production was gradual. Domestic woollen spinning continued until the introduction of the 'mule' in the 1830s. Power-loom weaving caused the fragile woollen yarn to break easily and power looms were not taken up by the woollen industry until after 1850. Resistance to change meant the survival of handloom weaving into the early twentieth century. Timmy Feather of Buckley Green Bottom, Stanbury, is thought to have been the last working handloom-weaver in West Yorkshire.

Harnessing water power to the new spinning machinery in woollen manufacture came thirty years after water-powered worsted spinning, that is during the 1820s. Woollen weaving by water power soon followed and consequently weaving sheds tended to be added to existing woollen spinning mills. As a result, integration of these two processes under one roof became a feature of Yorkshire woollen manufacure whereas the worsted industry maintained a high degree of segregation throughout the nineteenth century. The replacement of water power by the more efficient method of steam power in the case of the woollen industry did not occur until the 1830s and by the 1850s in the upper Calder Valley. **(23)** Even then, water horse-power capacity did not fall quantitatively.

West Riding Woollen Mills

	Total Horse Power	Steam H.P.	Water H.P.	% Water H.P. to Total
1836	8890	6218	2672	30.2
1839	9682	7191	2491	25.7
1845	10390	8080	2310	22.2
1850	11753	9047	2706	22.9

In the early days of steam power, large supplies of coal were needed to power the engines and only those communities blessed with their own coal seams or transport systems providing cheap coal made the transition to steam power. In the remote valleys of upland Calderdale, domestic weaving and water-powered spinning survived well into the second half of the nineteenth century. Steam eventually overtook them but at Lumb Mill, Wainstalls, high in the Calder Valley, machinery was driven by a water-wheel until 1953. **(18)**

The Nineteenth Century —
A Golden Age of Wool Manufacturing

The coming of steam power centralised textile production in a handful of urban areas — Leeds, Halifax, Bradford, Huddersfield, Dewsbury and Keighley, in addition to smaller 'fringe' centres at Brighouse, Bingley, Batley, Cleckheaton and Shipley. Moreover during the nineteenth century these textile centres came to offer a wide range of different qualities and types of cloth, each town specialising in a specific kind of cloth. This geographical specialisation was much more diverse than simply the distinction between woollens and worsteds.

Heavy woollen manufacturing including the 'mungo and shoddy' trades (the mixture of wool with old woollen or worsted rags, such as stockings, flannels, etc.) (77) came to be centred upon Dewsbury, Batley, Morley and the Spen Valley. The Huddersfield manufacturers developed a reputation as fancy woollen specialists, whereas Saddleworth specialised in shawls and flannels. The Upper Calder valley around Elland, Luddenden and Mytholmroyd went in for the manufacture of blankets. In the worsted region around Bradford and Keighley, townships were famed for women's dress goods whilst Bradford itself concentrated upon fine worsteds. Around Halifax men's suitings were favoured and in the centre of Halifax heavy worsteds and woollen carpet manufacturing became established. Leeds continued to produce fine quality woollens. Such specialisation was probably begun by two or three firms having success in pioneering and developing new brands of wool textiles. The best examples of this are the alpaca and mohair trades in the Bradford worsted trade and the establishment of the tweed industry in the Colne Valley. In the former, Titus Salt and John Foster at Black Dyke Mills, Queensbury, (25) enjoyed almost a monopoly of alpaca cloth before others followed their lucrative examples. In the Colne Valley the firm of W. E. Crowther & Sons pioneered a business in fine quality ladies' tweeds which Lockwoods, Mallinsons and other firms quickly followed.

Within these regions, firms competed to produce standardised goods in large quantities at unit profit rates. There was, however, particularly in the worsted ladies' dress trade, the opportunity to 'make a killing' in the market by anticipating 'frock fashion' and acquiring in advance the colour and designs of the forthcoming season's fashions. The success and superiority of the mixed worsted trade in Bradford caused a harmful complacency in the field of textile design. Several unsuccessful attempts were made to establish a 'design school' in Bradford but by 1862 a correspondent to the Bradford Observer could write:

> 'generally our designers do not stand very high — they understand copying better than originating'

Bradford Technical College

and nothing was done until the opening of the Bradford Technical College in 1879, by which time it was too late.

One can hardly blame members of Bradford's Chamber of Commerce for not seeing the advantages of technical education when their business was so brisk, their profits so high and their goods in such great demand. They preferred to work to finely calculated profit margins by selling 'bread and butter cloths' in very large quantities. In that context, profit depended largely upon the low cost input of labour and raw materials. The latter could be got round by subtle blending of fibres and company blend books contained highly-kept industrial secrets, the details of which were sometimes kept in code. Consequently the price and supply of raw wool was crucial to the fortunes of all. Choosing the right wool for the right product at the cheapest price raised the status of the woolsorter in both the woollen and worsted industries of the nineteenth century. There were only so many English sheep and a sudden increase in demand caused wool prices to rise dramatically. The importance of the wool price in costing the final product explains the crucial importance of wool selection and the high value which employers placed upon their woolsorters. (47) Also, the fluctuating nature of the raw wool market caused some manufacturers to do something about the supply of raw material by establishing the Wool Supply Association in February 1859.

Long stapled English wool was not appropriate to the short-stapled needs of Yorkshire woollen manufacturers and increasingly they looked abroad for their supply. Imports came initially from Spain and Germany but by 1870 Australia supplied 175 million pounds of our 263 million pounds of imported raw wool and led to regular colonial wool sales in London after 1835. Colonial wool growers sent their wool to brokers in England but after 1880 wool was sold at auctions in Melbourne, Sydney, Adelaide and Geelong as a result of improvements in transport and communications (the world-wide telegraph system). This meant that English wool staplers needed to be represented at the Australian auctions. This trend worked against the small Yorkshire wool stapler, many of whom went out of business about this time. Wool dealing fell into the hands of a few large merchants and manufacturers centred in buildings like the Bradford Wool Exchange, built in 1864. (28) There, in the magnificent Gothic structure in Market Street, assembled buyers and merchants from all over the world. Once upon a time Bradford could boast there was not a type of wool or hair, no matter where grown, for which a buyer could not be found on the Exchange.(30) Its members were truly international as Bradford's own J. B. Priestley noted in his autobiographical writings:

> 'Some of its citizens went regularly to the other side of the globe to buy wool. Others went abroad, from Belgium to China selling yarn and pieces. They returned to Market Street, the same sturdy Bradfordians, from the ends of the earth. You used to meet men who did not look as if they had ever been further than York or Morecambe but who actually knew every continental express'. *English Journey* (1933).

Buying wool at the right time crucially determined the price of the end product and the overall profitabiity of a firm. Woollen manufacturers continued to buy their own wool direct from the wool merchant but this was less true of the worsted industry where the topmaker made an appearance in the late 1870s. The topmaker bought wool, sorted it and usually had it combed by firms of commission combers who combed the wool for a fixed rate of payment and returned the tops, noil and waste to the topmaker, who then supplied the spinner with ready-to-use worsted tops. This system shortened the time between which the spinner purchased his raw material and when he sold the finished yarn, vital in a system of complex credit terms. This popularised topmaking after 1875 and in consequence many of the old wool staplers became topmakers.

As we have seen the introduction of machinery and the coming of the factory system was well advanced in both branches of the Yorkshire wool textile industry by 1860, although worsted manufactures were swifter than their woollen counterparts to complete the conversion from domestic/manual production to mechanised factory methods. Power-loom weaving came more slowly to woollen manufacturers particularly in the fancy woollen trade around Huddersfield. Even steam-powered mule spinning (53) was only gradually taken up by the woollen industry where there was still much to be done by 1865 and yet the worsted industry had completely mechanised its spinning process by 1830.

The speed and efficiency by which the worsted trade adapted to new methods is best seen in the replacement of hand-combing by the introduction of the 'nip' combing machine in 1845. George Donnisthorpe, a Leeds mechanic, had been employed by Samuel Cunliffe Lister who had taken out the first patent for 'square motion' combing in 1838. Lister and Donnisthorpe went on to buy up most other wool combing patents and finally marketed their machine for £1,200 each (a profit of £1,000 per machine). Overnight, Lister had a virtual monopoly of mechanised combing which created great wealth and later allowed him to build the magnificent Lister mill at Manningham. **(40)** By 1860 the hand combers were described as 'almost extinct as an industrial class' so swift and widespread had been the adoption of mechanised combing in the Bradford worsted trade. Full mechanisation of both worsted and woollen manufacture had profound implications for the size of factories and the amount of money invested into fixed capital assets like the mills. Those built during the 1850s were unprecedentedly large; the Bowling Green Mill at Bingley was built by S. Wildman & Son to spin yarn on 25,000 spindles. **(24)** Titus Salt's mill at Saltaire was the largest mill in Europe in 1853 with a weaving shed containing 1,200 looms and where three thousand people were employed at one time. **(35)**

Wool Dyeing

The one process where there was little evidence of improvement in the 'age of progress' was in the dyeing of wool textile fabrics. **(69)** Woad and various vegetable sources of dyes were still used, even after Perkins' discovery of aniline dyes in 1856. West Yorkshire dyers excused themselves in the slow up-take of aniline dyes by arguing that they were never paid enough by manufacturers to allow them to develop dyeing as a science, and it was in connection with this problem that pressure grew for the industry to develop technical education in West Yorkshire, similar to the systems in France and Germany.

Warehouses and Merchanting

Another significant development in textile history during the nineteenth century and one which can be easily discerned in many West Yorkshire 'townscapes' was the profound change in the merchanting of woven cloth. Until 1830, the Cloth and Piece Halls of West Yorkshire had been the market place for the sale of finished goods. As the domestic system and its small independent clothiers became a thing of the past so did the distributive system which had supported it. Cloth Hall cubicles and trestle-tables were no longer appropriate for the increasingly capitalised and highly competitive industry based on factory production. After 1830 an increasing number of woollen and worsted manufacturers and merchants began to build their own warehouses in the town centres and close to their place of manufacture. Until 1850 these warehouses consisted of 'an untidy arrangement of sheds' but the home-trade warehouse of Robert Milligan in Bradford (now the Telegraph & Argus building) and the magnificence of the buildings at Saltaire set new architectural standards after 1853. Other manufacturers followed the example of Salt and Milligan in Bradford and architecturally-designed warehouses sprang up all over West Yorkshire, increasing in scale and

Milligans Warehouse, Bradford

grandeur as the century proceeded. The best surviving examples of this retailing revolution are to be found in Bradford's unique warehousing precinct of 'Little Germany' so called because of its association with numerous German merchanting families who tranferred their business to Bradford after 1830. **(39)**

Factory System

The coming of machinery and steam power to woollen textile production has been described as the 'industrial revolution' but as we have seen, such changes did not come as dramatically as that term implies but came gradually, at different times and at a different pace to various branches of the industry. Even so, to the employees of the first half of the nineteenth century, the degree and pace of change was too profound and at a time when there was no welfare state to cushion them against unemployment, hardship and even starvation. As thousands poured into the textile towns from the countryside around, the transition to urban living and factory work came as a traumatic experience for many textile workers used to open-space, working at their own pace and living in a culture that was largely rural, slow yet secure. By 1830, there were few laws about public health and factory conditions. Life in towns like Bradford, Huddersfield and Leeds was new in human experience.

Later generations, with the benefit of hindsight, were horrified by the conditions under which men and women worked in the new factories (some of them converted corn mills). Actions and conditions that seem brutal and harsh to us now were not necessarily so, at the time. Millowners and employers did not know any better; they were in charge of a work system that was completely unprecedented. Of all the harmful consequences of the factory system, the employment of the very young was perhaps the most controversial. The long hours, (anything upto 13 hours a day) and tiring work of factory children were particularly iniquitous in Bradford which led one government official to describe the town:

> 'as a place where we should find a greater number of cripples with shorter hours. That is certainly correct so far as regards the greater number of cripples but the regular hours at Bradford appear to be at least an hour longer than at Leeds and the practice of taking very young children seems to have prevailed in a much greater degree . . .'

Children were beaten to stay awake, were forced to walk to work in bare feet early on cold winter mornings. Many, like young William Pickles of Wilsden, grew up stunted and crippled. Orphans from London workhouses were 'apprenticed' to Yorkshire factory owners as virtual slaves by their parish authorities. Having contributed significantly to one of the most abominable social evils, some enlightened Bradford owners at least inaugurated the movement to abolish child labour in their factories. Men like John Wood and Richard Oastler petitioned parliament to stop child employment in mills, to cut down the hours of adults and generally to improve working conditions in mills and factories.

Apart from child labour, some workpeople also resented the loss of independence and self-respect which went with factory work. William Illingworth of Idle preferred,

Oastler statue, Bradford

> 'having work in our own houses to going out with it . . . we can begin
> soon or late . . . and those that have families have an opportunity in
> one way or another of training them up in some little thing . . .'

Easing the workforce into the new work ethos was a management responsibility of the first generation of factory owners. Early factories resembled, both in physical appearance and internal administration, the parish workhouses and operatives found it difficult to adjust to working in them. Attendance at the mills in the early days was very irregular. Men still took time off work to do the autumn harvest. Manufacturers frequently suffered on the first day of the working week 'St. Monday' when employees extended their day of rest. 'Wakes' weeks also brought their usual toll of absenteeism and truancy. In 1806 R. Cookson, a Leeds manufacturer, found

> 'the utmost distaste on the part of the men to any regular hours or
> habits. the men themselves were considerably dissatisfied because
> they could not go in and out as they pleased . . .'

Consequently factory owners came to insist on a strict factory discipline of long hours and minimum wages. Lateness, drunkenness, talking and sleeping on the job were punished by fines or even corporal punishment for children. The interests of individual workpeople became subordinate to the whole working unit, the mill. The trauma experienced by the early generation of millworkers was aggravated by the threat from the improved technology of new machines.

The most famous rejection of automation subsequently became a byword for any refusal to accept innovation — Luddism. In 1811/12 croppers in the Yorkshire woollen industry openly rebelled against rising prices and the introduction of shearing frames which had replaced the huge hand shears of the cropper (17); these frames were first used at Bradley Mills in Huddersfield in 1800. Luddism, a secret society, is said to have originated in Nottingham but the chief Luddite in West Yorkshire was George Mellor, a hand-cropper of Longroyd Bridge near Huddersfield. Mellor and others met at the Shears Inn, Hightown and from there plotted to smash shearing frames all over Hartshead Moor. (16) In April 1812 an angry mob of 'Luddites' attacked William Cartwright's mill at Rawfolds and at the end of that month another manufacturer, William Horsfall of Marsden, was shot dead on Crosland Moor. Mellor and his three accomplices went to the gallows at York Castle in January 1813 along with thirteen other Yorkshire Luddites. Later, violence and machine-smashing marked the introduction of power looms in Airedale in 1822 and of mechanical combing in Bradford in 1825/6. In 1842 and 1848 unemployed handcombers, under the banner of Chartism, threatened revolution throughout West Yorkshire. A new kind of society was emerging in a Yorkshire where the old techniques of social living were in decay.

Early efforts to shore up the traditional economic and social relationships of the domestic system included attempts on the part of some millowners to recreate, in the urban context, some of the mental and moral conditions of the closely-knit and interdependent, rural community of pre-factory times. Early millowners tried to translate the discipline and culture of village organisation to the working conditions of the urban environment by better housing accommodation close to the mill; by the provision of education in the shape of factory schools and institutes for working men. Self-expression and recreation were encouraged as antidotes to drunkenness and brawling as firms financed and promoted their own brass bands, choirs and horticultural societies. The logical conclusion of this need to harmonise class relationships and reconcile the division between Capital and Labour took the form of the 'industrial village' run on paternalist lines. Edward Akroyd, a Halifax manufacturer, built the village of Copley in 1850 and over many years the Horsfall family provided many facets of village life around their mill at Addingham.

Copley village, near Halifax

By far the best and most advanced example of a factory village is the well known complex at Saltaire with its magnificent worsted mill, eight hundred workpeople's cottages, almshouses and a whole range of public buildings in the lower reaches of the Aire valley, and nestling beneath Baildon Moor and Shipley Glen. **(33)** Its streets, laid out to an orderly grid pattern, are named after the founder, Titus Salt and his family. Salt was a successful and wealthy worsted manufacturer who made a fortune in the Bradford worsted trade, from pioneering the use of alpaca, the fleece of the South American llama. Apart from one or two public buildings the village is litle altered, in the physical sense since its erection between 1850 and 1870. The Salt family is no longer connected with the mill which was until recently, part of the Illingworth Morris group of companies. They ceased manufacturing at the mill in 1985 and the future of this magnificent Victorian mill is now in doubt. However, whilst it stands it serves as a reminder of Salt's efforts to mould the security and order of pre-industrial village life on to the impersonal and disordered urban culture of the industrial capitalist society of the nineteenth century. The mill's magnificent six-storeyed southern front also reminds us of the vast wealth and entrepreneurial success that it was possible to achieve in the wool trade of nineteenth century Yorkshire. **(32)**

Saltaire and other industrial empires like it reflect the 'boom' conditions of the wool textile industry up to 1874. Thereafter, profits did not come so easily. The mid-century years of confidence gave way in the last quarter of the century to a period of doubt, recrimination and gloom.

The Years of Contraction: 1890–1980

Much of what was wrong with Yorkshire's wool textile industry in the first quarter of the twentieth century has its origins in the heady years of Victorian prosperity. During the last decades of the nineteenth century the industry had to weather changes in fashion, textile design and wool supply but perhaps the most damaging of all its problems after 1874 was the world shift to protection in the form of prohibitive tariffs. Various West Yorkshire chambers of commerce had opposed this trend with some success up to 1870 but thereafter, one by one, European and American markets became enveloped by tariff barriers. France, Germany, Austria–Hungary all closed their doors to English woollen exports, particularly woven cloths, during the 1870s. Finally, the McKinley Tariff of 1895 halved woollen and worsted cloth exports to the U.S.A. and it was predicted that grass would grow in the streets of Bradford. Thereafter, there was a decline in the relative importance of wool manufactures to total British exports, falling from 13% in 1874 to 9% in 1914. After the First World War output fell further but recovered during the 1930s. The export of tops and spun yarn, however, remained stable as consuming nations were finally providing their own textile requirements and were becoming increasingly self-sufficient, particularly in the weaving sector. Britain's share in this diminishing volume of world trade in woollen goods was precariously maintained until the financial crash of 1929. During the economic slump which followed, Yorkshire exports in wool tissues dropped sharply though less so in tops and yarn.

Indices of Exports of Tops, Yarns and Tissues, by weight
1928 = 100

Year	World Exports of			United Kingdom Exports of		
	Tops	Yarns	Tissues	Tops	Yarns	Tissues
1928	100	100	100	100	100	100
1929	92	97	96	97	96	91
1930	89	87	78	85	76	68
1931	95	82	65	82	72	51
1932	95	56	43	124	78	47
1933	108	63	46	135	88	54
1934	91	61	49	124	88	59
1935	103	58	49	165	84	63
1936	99	59	53	153	76	68
1937	93	59	62	117	65	71
1938	83	54	52	97	57	54

Source: Imperial Economic Committee and "Facts and Figures"

Market losses in the Far East, where good trade had been done in heavier and cheaper cloths, were particularly damaging to the Heavy Woollen District of Dewsbury, Morley and the Spen Valley, where numerous mills closed down in the 1930s. Unemployment in the industry reached its peak (37%) in 1931; between 1912 and 1937, 30,000 jobs were lost in the West Yorkshire wool industry (11% of the total workforce). Even this compared favourably with the Lancashire cotton industry in the same period, where job losses totalled 260,000 (42%) and where there was limited alternative employment.

The Yorkshire industry had always been heavily dependent on women and juveniles, particularly in worsted spinning. (55) In the woollen sector, men and women were employed in equal numbers although wool sorting and combing remained largely male occupations. (47)

Employment in the UK Wool Textile Industry

	Men (000's)	Women (000's)	Total (000's)	Index of Employment	Proportion under 18 years
1907	112.3	147.6	259.9 }	100	20.7
1912	121.7	157.9	279.6 }		22.2
1924	119.0	157.5	276.5	102	17.0
1930	97.6	132.7	230.3	85	15.1
1933	100.3	135.3	235.6	87	12.8
1935	104.7	137.5	242.2	90	14.8
1937	108.1	141.8	249.9	92	17.6

Source: "Facts and Figures" (issued by The National Wool Textile Export Corporation in 1944). Based on Census of Production and I.D.A.C. Inquiries.

By 1935 when something of a recovery was on the way the number of persons employed in the woollen sector was 83,000 and 120,000 in the worsted sector.

This 'shake-out' of the labour force and the modernisation of machinery after 1920 made the industry more competitive and contributed to a temporary recovery after 1935, thanks largely to an increased home demand for woollen goods. This had been constant during the difficult years following the 1914–18 war but had increased dramatically when foreign woollen imports were unable to compete in this country following the depreciation of sterling and the imposition of 50% import duties in 1931. The absence of foreign wool textiles on the British market led to a noticeable increase in the output of West Yorkshire mills. This expansion of the home market was further fuelled by an improvement in the real incomes of British consumers. Some mills which had been almost derelict found a new lease of life. In particular, worsted yarn spinners got back on their feet with the aid of the British hosiery industry which bought roughly half of the total Yorkshire worsted yarn output in 1937. It was during these years of flagging trade that wool scourers experimented with sulphuric acid in the extraction of wool fat from the scouring water sent into city sewers. Perhaps the best known West Yorkshire sewage recovery plant was developed by Bradford Corporation on the Esholt Hall estate. (81) Here, grease was recovered and sold in its crude state; other by-products of oils and soap were made profitable by the industry in these years.

Yarn exports failed to experience the same kind of recovery owing to the demise of the German market. Between 1909–1913 Germany had taken 55 million pounds of our total yarn production of 87 million pounds; by 1936–38 this had fallen to only 8 million pounds.

Production of Tops, Yarns and Tissues

	Output of Tops		Output of Yarn		Output of Tissues[1]	
	Million lbs.	Index	Million lbs.	Index	Million sq. yads	Index
1907	243.5	100	446.0	100	454.7	100
1912	304.5		565.1		481.0	
1924	285.5	104	554.5	110	475.7	84
1930	224.5	82	385.9	76	343.9	61
1933	309.5	113	522.0	103	413.3	73
1934	274.8	100	519.2	103	420.8	74
1935	307.5	112	543.0	108	439.2	78
1937	278.5	102	565.8	112	474.6	84

[1] Figures for 1907 and 1912 are in linear yards, but adjusted approximately to sq. yds. in the index in the final column.

Source "Facts and Figures"

The net effect of all these structural changes enabled each section of the industry to restore productivity by 1937 very close to that of 1924. The ground lost during the depression years had been largely recovered by 1937 in a world where the trade in woollen goods was continuously contracting.

During the Second World War the revived West Yorkshire wool textile industry was deliberately run down by government policies designed to transfer resources and labour into the armed forces or into more strategic industries. Exports were negligible during the war and the labour force dropped by 32% between 1937 and 1944. After 1945 recovery was inevitably hampered by a severe shortage of labour, particularly of women. In view of this, some firms considered moving out of the region to Darlington, Belfast, Lanarkshire and even to the South Yorkshire Coalfield where there was a residue of female labour. Some firms transported female workers from Rotherham and accommodated them during the working week. The solution to the industry's labour problem ultimately lay with the employment of East European immigrants and, after 1955, with the large-scale employment of Asians from Pakistan and India.

After 1950 millowners in West Yorkshire were also having to compete in the labour market with newer and faster growing industries offering higher wages, better conditions and greater security. Parents of juveniles, on whom the industry relied heavily (21% of all those employed in 1907 and 18% thirty years later), were reluctant to put their children into an industry which had experienced such dark and insecure days in their own lifetimes. As a result, firms had to pay wages considerably higher than some of their European and Asiatic counterparts. These competitors were able to produce and market goods in Britain after 1952 at a much lower price than that of the West Yorkshire manufacturers.

The removal of the import duties on foreign yarn and fabrics exposed the industry's home market to the icy blast of foreign competition. From 1957 there followed another period of contraction which saw many old established family businesses disappear and their mills close. The vandalised graves of men like Isaac Holden, Christopher Waud, Jacob Behrens and Robert Milligan at Undercliffe Cemetery, Bradford, **(95)** are a sad symbol of the many fine business empires which disappeared from the West Yorkshire scene in the early 1960s; their derelict and depressed mills converted to furniture and carpet warehouses, churches, temples and the ultimate insult for Saltaire Mill — the possibility of becoming a museum of textile industry! **(86)**

The Wool Industry of Today

The contraction of the late 1950s continued into the next decade as the 1,123 Yorkshire woollen or worsted mills of 1950 shrank to 825 by 1967. In the same period the number of spindles in use in the county fell by 30% with the number of power looms slipping by 43%. During this period the heavy industry of Morley and Dewsbury almost disappeared owing to the increased demand for lighter clothes as a result of the introduction of domestic central heating and car heating. The greatest blow to West Yorkshire's heavy woollen industry, however, came from cheap Italian imports of heavy woollen skirtings and coatings, particularly from Prato near Florence where the virtual cottage industry of family labour and low labour costs enabled the Italians to undersell Yorkshire heavy woollen manufactures, even in this country.

Despite a brief recovery at the end of the 1960s when the industry was beginning to adjust to the market's demand for more casual wear, the decline continued as a result of the international oil crisis of 1974. Thereafter, the world economic crisis of 1979–81 coincided with a wool crisis and caused even more textile firms to go under. Since the war, some large cloth manufacturers had switched to worsted spinning by taking over small firms and reoccupying closed mills. Perhaps the best known of these textile giants is the Bradford-based worsted combing and spinning firm of Illingworth & Morris PLC. Even this large company had accrued borrowings of over £20 million by 1982 and was in danger of bankruptcy. Today it and the wool textile industry is undergoing something of a recovery. Shrinkage and contraction since 1950 have left it more competitive, more specialised and better equipped to meet the consumer demands of the high-street retailers. Fashion yarns in wool have been joined by the production of blended and synthetic knitwear yarns manufactured directly for the major high street multiple stores like Jaeger, Burtons and Marks & Spencer.

Perhaps the most beneficial development of recent years has been in the design of yarns to meet the fashion trends in markets throughout the world. The textile designer is no longer one of the backroom boys but meets the customer direct, providing (by use of computer) colour and design themes eighteen months in advance of their appearance in shop windows. These seasonal colour and design themes are then followed up by spinning companies in their individual collections which range from acrylic blends through pure new wool 'superwash' to mohair rich qualities; from angora style and cotton look to glitter yarns in various counts. One Bradford spinning mill alone produces enough yarn to make half a million knitted garments each week.

At the top end of the market the industry continues to manufacture high quality all-wool worsted cloth. Much of this is now made by Huddersfield firms such as the Allied Textiles group who produce largely for the export markets of Japan, USA and Europe. The raw material for these fine quality worsteds is no longer bought and sold at the Bradford Wool Exchange. The clamour and activity of 'change days', when the heads of small family textile firms made a special occasion of coming into Bradford to see their bank manager, topmaker or solicitor, have now gone. (30) Topmakers and top merchants had well nigh disappeared by the 1960s and the improvement in telecommunications facilitated private purchases of raw wool and signalled the demise of the Bradford Wool Exchange. Even so, wool auctions are still held at the British Wool Marketing Board's premises at Clayton. (44)

Other expensive natural fibres such as cashmere, mohair and silk continue to be used in the industry in addition to the large synthetic output, and Bradford firms like Hields and John Foster continue to thrive on their exports of fine worsted cloth. As well as fabric for clothes, Yorkshire mills make cloth for billiard tables, tennis balls and transport seating. Yarn spinning for the carpet industry has developed as another specialist sector of the industry, exporting £40 million of carpet yarn in 1985. Yarn output has advanced quickly in recent years as a result of increased capital investment and a continued up-dating of machinery, particularly the introduction of the 'self-twist' spinning machine.

It is still imperative that the industry retains a lion's share of the home market and continues to compete there with foreign imports. The level of textile consumption in the United Kingdom has risen yearly since 1982 and Yorkshire's wool textile industry has shared in this boom owing to firms' close liaison with the major retailing outlets and to their more market-oriented approach to business.

In the export field, the value of wool textile exports has grown steadily since 1982 in spite of high tariff barriers in places like South Korea, Taiwan and Brazil. Fluctuations in our exchange rates coupled with a high rate of inflation have diminished the competitiveness of British textile exports and undermined the true export potential of the industry in recent years.

The shake out of the labour force of the 1960s (1951=150,000; 1968=40,000) has continued with the further rationalisation of the industry. In terms of employment the industry really cannot get any smaller. In 1986 there were 125 woollen spinning and 62 worsted spinning mills in the United Kingdom, most of them in West Yorkshire, with 172 weaving mills (5,332 looms). The industry now employs around 40,000 people and still employs large numbers of women and ethnic minority groups. Recruitment into the industry is organised in a more professional way than ever before. A retraining committee of the Confederation of British Wool Textiles now runs a career-structured scheme for two hundred young trainee managers with four textile training boards in Huddersfield, Bradford, Halifax and Otley. The industry also runs a Youth Training scheme for factory operatives and is conscious of the need for training people at all levels in readiness for the 1990s and beyond. In this and so many other ways the Yorkshire wool textile industry of today is beginning to create an environment in which an entrepreneur like Titus Salt or Samuel Lister might, yet again, exploit his business talents and take the industry to new heights of prosperity.

Gary Firth

1   Bronze Age stone circle, near Kilnsey

These eerie monoliths form part of an ancient stone circle high in the limestone hills of Craven; they were part of an early Bronze Age culture which also included rudimentary clothmaking by means of spindle whorls and upright looms.

2 Abandoned mill stone, Addingham Moorside, in Wharfedale
This is one of several millstones littered around the moor in this area. They were originally intended as part of the machinery of local corn mills, the buildings of which were initially adapted to the large scale production of wool textiles. Hence, the early association of the word 'mill' with the making of cloth.

3   Mastiles Lane, near Kilnsey

The monks of Fountains established a grange at Kilnsey from which the sheep farms of Malham Moor were managed. They also owned property in Malham village which housed a steward, and they were owners of several houses on the moorland of this photograph, in which three or four shepherds lived. Mastiles Lane was the 'drove road' linking Kilnsey with Malham.

4   Brimham Rocks, near Pateley Bridge, Nidderdale

Standing like some Gothic ruins these huge masses of millstone grit offered ideal shelter for breeds of Yorkshire sheep like the Penistone. Eroded by winds since Permian times, these spectacular shaped rocks are each individually named. Brimham was another of the large estates owned and farmed by the monks of Fountains Abbey.

5 Fountains Abbey at dusk

Under the monastic rule after 1130 much poor land in West Yorkshire was brought back into cultivation, forests cleared, marshes drained and roads built. The Cistercian abbey at Fountains, 2½ miles west of Ripon, is thought to be the finest of Yorkshire's monastic houses. It was founded in 1132 by thirteen monks from St. Mary's Abbey in York. Like most orders, the Cistercians soon came to have an interest in trade despite their supposed ascetic way of life.

6   The Cellarium, Fountains Abbey

The main income of the Cistercians was their international wool crop which went largely to the merchants of Lombardy. Fleeces not exported directly abroad were stored here in the cellarium at Fountains (approximately 100 metres long). There are twenty-two bays divided down the middle by a row of arches supported on columns. The last twelve bays formed the refectory where the lay brothers lived and ate but the rest were used for storage of wool.

7 Rievaulx Abbey, North Yorkshire

Another Cistercian house which owned extensive estates across North Yorkshire and grazed thousands of sheep upon its acres. It was founded in 1131 by Walter Espec. Here the surviving portions of the nave and choir walls contain exquisite stonework similar to that at Whitby and Kirkstall.

8   Merchant Adventurers' Hall, York

Perhaps one of the finest medieval buildings in the North of England, the earliest part dates back to the late fourteenth century when it was founded by one of the city trade guilds. By 1430 it belonged to the Guild of the Craft of Mercers which, by 1580, had been reconstituted as the Society of Merchant Adventurers who did much to promote the English cloth trade all over the known world in medieval times.

9 Interior of the Merchant Adventurers' Hall, York
The building still hosts the ancient courts and a service is held in the chapel of this hall each year. Heading the Adventurers' roll of honour is William Wooller, cloth merchant of Airedale (died 1597).

10 Combshop, Addingham Moorside

This outbuilding at Hardwicke Hall farm, Addingham Moorside, is reputed to be a combshop of the pre-factory era of worsted cloth production. Here, handcombers practised their specialist but unhealthy occupation separating woollen tops from noils. The proximity of the farm and the rural character of the surrounding environment demonstrates the close association of pre-industrial cloth production with agriculture.

11 Handcombing — detail from S. C. Lister monument, Lister Park, Bradford

This detail in bronze is from the pediment of Samuel Cunliffe Lister's statue in Lister Park, Manningham and clearly shows the traditional skill of combing wool by hand. The wool comber used two heavy combs, each with numerous metal prongs which were heated in charcoal-fuelled pots. One comb was attached to a beam in this unhealthy cottage industry and the other was used to draw out the wool from it, separating the short fibres from the long to create a sliver. The short fibred wool, known as noils, was discarded but about twenty slivers were made into a 'top', the spinners' basic material.

12 Loomshop, Addingham

This building represents the wool textile industry on the threshold of factory production. Small independent clothiers extended their farm buildings by a single cell loomshop of two storeys but John Cockshott of Addingham was a substantial master manufacturer (a forerunner of the factory owner) and was able to erect this free standing loomshop with accommodation for 62 looms. This building signalled the beginning of the end of domestic production, the weaver's house no longer being also his place of work.

13 Weavers' cottage at Golcar

In spite of the appearance of the loomshop (1790s) and, soon after, the factory, much of West Yorkshire's woollen cloth continued to be made up in the weavers' homes until well into the nineteenth century. The West Yorkshire landscape is well known for its weavers' cottages; often terraced rows of two or three storey houses, identified by their numerous long mullioned loomshop windows like these at Golcar which were built into the hillside and where the work area had a separate access (at the rear) on the second floor.

14   Tenterfield, Pig Hill Wood, near Huddersfield ▲

For many centuries woven cloth was dried in the open air by means of stretching it on a tenter seam or tenter hooks (hence the phrase 'to be on tenterhooks'). Here are possibly the last surviving hooks fixed to the weaver's cottage and stretched to these tenter posts at the end of each cottage garden (three in all).

15   Piece Hall Yard, Halifax ▶

So named because of the lengths (pieces) of finished cloth which were sold from its 315 merchants' rooms. It was built in 1779 at a time when it was impossible for prospective buyers to visit the many thousands of Yorkshire weavers' cottages where cloth was woven. Still very much as it was, the classical architecture and colonnaded galleries now house an art gallery, museum and numerous craft shops.

16   Marsden Moor, Huddersfield

This is the desolate and windswept landscape of Luddite country for it was in this region that Ned Ludd found much support for his machine breaking activities in 1811/12. It was at Marsden that William Horsfall employed 400 workers in his mill where he introduced the new shearing frames which threatened the livelihood of the handcroppers. On Tuesday, 8th April, 1812 Horsfall was passing terrain like this on his journey from Huddersfield to Marsden when two assassins fired at him from behind a drystone wall. Horsfall's death, and the attack on Rawfolds mill, ultimately led to the leading 17 Luddites being hanged at York in the following year.

17 Cropping shears, Bradford Industrial Museum
These large and heavy hand shears cropped the nap of the woven cloth to produce a smooth finish. It was the mechanisation of this finishing process which threatened the Yorkshire croppers or 'shearmen' and frightened many of them into the ranks of the Luddites.

18   Disused water-wheel, Lumb Mill, Wainstalls, near Halifax

Once Yorkshire manufacturers had decided to turn away from domestic production and increase their output of woollen yarn by harnessing the new machines to a new source of power, they looked to the water courses in the deans and cloughs of the Pennine hills. Consequently the first factory system was very much a part of the countryside and only with the coming of steam was factory production associated with intensive urbanisation. This surviving cast iron drive wheel (36 feet diameter) belonged to the Lumb Mill water-wheel at Wainstalls, high in the Calder Valley where seven other similar mills were all owned by the Calvert family. Erected in 1803 it was the mill's sole source of power until electrification in 1953.

19   Bents Mill (1799) near Harden

This water-powered spinning mill is one of five spinning mills built on this stretch of the beck at Harden in the last decade of the eighteenth century. Adjacent to it was Hallas Bridge Mill, another 'undershot' water-wheel mill of the same period. Initially they were built to manufacture cotton goods but converted to the production of worsted yarn after the Napoleonic Wars. The water-wheels have been removed but the mill dams survive.

◀ **20 Bents Mill, near Harden**

The roof beams of this early water-powered spinning mill, built in 1799 by William Wilkinson, were originally designed to provide extra storage space for raw wood and semi-manufactured goods.

▲ **21 Pecket Well Mill, Hebden Bridge**

Located on the Keighley–Hebden Bridge road (opened 1814), this small water-powered mill was built before the Napoleonic Wars to make fustian cloth. A whole village grew up around it.

22   Jumble Hole Clough, Hebden Bridge
Another water-powered cotton spinning mill of three storeys, built in an almost inaccessible location. Jumble Hole Clough runs from Blackshaw Head to Hebden Bridge and by 1840 accommodated four water-powered spinning mills, the goits and weirs of which still survive. This is what remains of Stamps Mill at the head of the clough and therefore the mill best served by the watercourse.

23   Lumb Mill chimney, Hebden Bridge
The replacement of water power by steam engines came gradually to different branches of the woollen and worsted industries. Those areas not blessed with their own supplies of coal or good transport systems were slow to take up steam power but even here in the remote Calder valley water-power at Lumb and Bob mills gave way to steam power after 1860 and the mill chimney became a feature of the Pennine countryside.

◀ 24 Bowling Green Mill, Bingley

During the nineteenth century, the amount of fixed capital invested in mills generally increased considerably in proportion to the increased scale of mill buildings. This enormous mill originally dwarfed the town of Bingley and the cottages surrounding it. Bowling Green mill was built by Samuel Wildman in 1871 and accommodated 25,000 worsted spindles.

▲ 25 John Foster's Black Dyke Mill, Queensbury, Bradford

This large and successful firm has long held a position of supremacy in the Bradford worsted trade. It was begun in 1819 by John Foster whose family ran Cannon Mill in Great Horton, Bradford, before building their own mill on the present site in 1835. Between 1835 and 1871 this family firm won numerous medals and awards at international textile fairs and exhibitions. With Titus Salt they shared in the promotion of alpaca and the profits therefrom have been ploughed back into a vast programme of rebuilding (Victoria and Shed mills). They remain one of the front runners in the production of fine quality worsted cloth.

26 Drummonds Mill, Bradford

The beauty and symmetry of these laminated wood arches belies the dangers such materials posed for workplaces where wool grease was everywhere. The bilingual message in the foreground leaves no doubt in anyone's minds of the fire hazard in textile mills.

27 John Foster's Black Dyke Mills, Queensbury, Bradford
Wealthy and progressive employers like Titus Salt and John Foster of Black Dyke Mills, Queensbury, installed light cast-iron pillars and beams in their mills to reduce the number of walls and thus increase a free flow of air.

28 Wool Exchange, Bradford

Roosting starlings survey the Gothic splendour of the clock tower of the Wool Exchange building in Market Street. In this building (erected in 1864) Bradfordians could boast there was not a type of wool or hair, no matter where grown, for which a buyer could not be found. Here the 150 feet high clock tower dominates the archway of the main entrance, flanked by the carved figures of Bishop Blaize, patron saint of woolcombers, and Edward III.

29 Cobden's statue, interior of Wool Exchange, Bradford

A founding father of free trade policies, Richard Cobden was paid the singular honour by the wool men of Bradford Chamber of Commerce when they commissioned this fine white marble statue to his memory. Cobden did much to open foreign markets to English wool goods after 1850. He stands between two capitals of polished granite each numbered to denote the 'selling' place of a particular wool merchant or top maker when this spacious hall teemed with wool dealers and manufacturers.

30   Interior — Wool Exchange, Bradford

Here C. M. Kelly, one of a handful of surviving members of the Wool Exchange, displays a photograph of busier days when the hall echoed to the calls of hundreds of competing merchants, topmakers and manufacturers.

31 Interior — Wool Exchange, Bradford

The spacious and imposing interior is dominated by an impressive hammer beam roof and the marble colonnades of the aisle arcade. The Exchange as such no longer trades and there are plans to convert it into a shopping mall.

32 Salts' Mill from the Congregational Chapel, Saltaire ▲

One of the biggest names in the Bradford worsted trade was Titus Salt whose five Bradford mills manufactured worsted cloth with alpaca and a cotton warp. In 1850 Salt rationalised his business affairs by moving out of Bradford to build the model industrial village of Saltaire. Between 1850 and 1853 this enormous six storey mill was built with all the finest architectural and engineering developments of the day. From the steps of his Congregational chapel there is a good view of the mill office block and boardroom. To the right is the workers' dining room. The chimney lost its 'Italianate cap' some years ago. On the roof of the south front of the mill perches a small Second World War machine gun turret in readiness for the Nazi invasion of the Aire Valley.

33 Albert Street, Saltaire ▶

Following the erection of Salts' mill, attention turned to the building of workpeople's cottages. When the scheme was completed in 1871 there were 22 streets of 850 houses plus 45 almshouses for the elderly. Albert Street, locally known as 't' Railway Bottom', was the northern boundary of the residential quarter of the village. Each cottage is stone built, lined with brick, and originally had a parlour, kitchen, pantry and two, three or four bedrooms depending on the individual family needs.

34   One of the last looms at Salts' Mill, Saltaire

In 1986, after 133 years of production, scrap metal merchants prepare to dismantle this pattern loom, one of the last in use at the mill.

35   Empty weaving shed, Salts' Mill, Saltaire
Nearly three thousand people thronged the original weaving shed at a banquet to celebrate the opening of Salts' mill in September 1853. It is now an empty shell, abandoned by its former glories.

36 'Snicket', Little Germany, Bradford
This narrow passageway in Bradford's warehousing precinct once echoed to the tramp of feet shod with clogs, as the worn millstone steps plainly testify.

37   Priestleys' Warehouse, Little Germany, Bradford
At 66 Vicar Lane, Bradford, this Victorian warehouse is outstanding for its simplicity of design, the work of Eli Milnes in 1867. Like many of Bradford's public and commercial buildings it has a prominent linear facade with each storey, all of which is capped with a heavy roof cornice. Through the high and grandious entrance passed numerous foreign merchants in search of the high-quality dress fabrics, for which Priestleys Ltd were famed.

38   Cast-iron gate, Law & Russell warehouse, Little Germany

39 Warehouses in Little Germany, Bradford

Until 1830 Cloth and Piece Halls had been the market place for finished goods, but as the domestic system and its small independent clothiers became a thing of the past so did the merchanting system which had supported them. After 1830 numerous German merchants moved from Leeds to Bradford to establish a unique warehousing precinct, still known as 'Little Germany'. To the right of the photograph is the entrance to De Vere House (1871). The large eagle over the doorway denotes the importance of the American market for the original owners, Thornton, Homan & Co. Opposite is the extravagantly designed warehouse of Law, Russell & Co designed by the architects of Saltaire, Lockwood & Mawson, in 1874.

40   'Lister's Pride', Lister's Mill, Bradford

This is the chimney of Lister's Mill, Bradford, an enormous worsted and silk manufactory originally with a total floor space of 26 acres. Its owner, Samuel Cunliffe Lister, had prospered as a result of his invention of the first effective woolcombing machine in 1845. The chimney, known as Lister's Pride, is 255 feet (78 metres) high and built in 1873 in the style of an Italian campanile or bell tower.

41 Interior, disused block, Lister's Mill, Bradford
With the contractions of the textile trade and the development of smaller and more efficient machinery many working mills no longer require vast multi-storey buildings.

42   Craghouse Farm, Addingham, near Ilkley
Sheep being herded in for shearing.

43   Shearing, Craghouse Farm, Addingham, near Ilkley
The sheep are sheared with electric shears in a matter of minutes and the fleeces are rolled into tight balls ready for collection by the British Wool Marketing Board.

44   Wool grading at British Wool Marketing Board, Clayton, Bradford
Here, huge bales of Southdown wool are being graded at the headquarters of the British Wool Marketing Board, Bradford.

◀ **45 Conditioning House, Bradford**
Wool absorbs or loses moisture from the atmosphere depending upon the different climate it is in, and in order to avoid disputes about wool weight ordered and wool weight delivered Bradford Corporation established an institution known as the Conditioning House. Its first premises were at the rear of the Town Hall, but in 1902 were transferred here to Cape Street, Bradford.

▲ **46 Wool bales at the Conditioning House, Bradford**
Consignments of wool like these await inspection and the issue of a certificate of 'condition' which are regarded as authoritative and impartial the world over.

47 Wool sorting at Lower Holme Mills, Baildon ▲

Each fleece contains numerous qualities of wool which are carefully sorted and divided by hand. The skilled wool sorter can distinguish the quality of the wool according to its length, fineness and crimp (waviness). The best wool is often found around the shoulders and on the back of the sheep.

48 Wool scouring, Whiteheads Mill, Bradford ▶

By this process the raw wool is washed to remove dirt, natural grease and vegetable impurities. Scouring produces the useful by-product of lanolin which is used in the manufacture of many soaps and cosmetics.

49   Card fettlers, Brackendale Spinning Co, Thackley, Bradford

Once the wool has been cleaned and scoured of dirt and grease, it can be disentangled and passed through a series of revolving cylinders called a carding machine. Originally this process was done by hand by means of two hand-sized boards fixed with fine metal pins, producing a short roll of wool known as a 'rolag'. The modern carding engine is one of the biggest in the industry and consists of a series of large cylinders and small rollers covered with tightly set wire teeth. Here two card fettlers set to, clearing the cylinders, a dirty and dangerous process now being overtaken by automation.

50 Lister Comb, Black Dyke Mill, Queensbury, Bradford

Combing is a distinct process in the making of worsted as opposed to woollen yarn. The combing machine straightens the wool, separating out the short fibres into an unwanted 'noil' and the longer fibres ('tops') into a long sliver. Here the 'nip' comb (patented by Samuel Cunliffe Lister in 1845) prepares to receive a series of card slivers.

51 Worsted 'Sinner', Daniel Illingworth's Mill, Bradford
The wool, once it has been drawn out to its required thickness (the count), is called a roving. The spinning process twists the fibres of the roving into a yarn which is wound on to a bobbin. Daniel Illingworth's mill is one of the largest spinners in the business and now forms part of the Illingworth Morris group.

52   Weaving sheds at Salts' Mill, Saltaire
The angled roofs were built facing north to provide maximum usage of daylight.

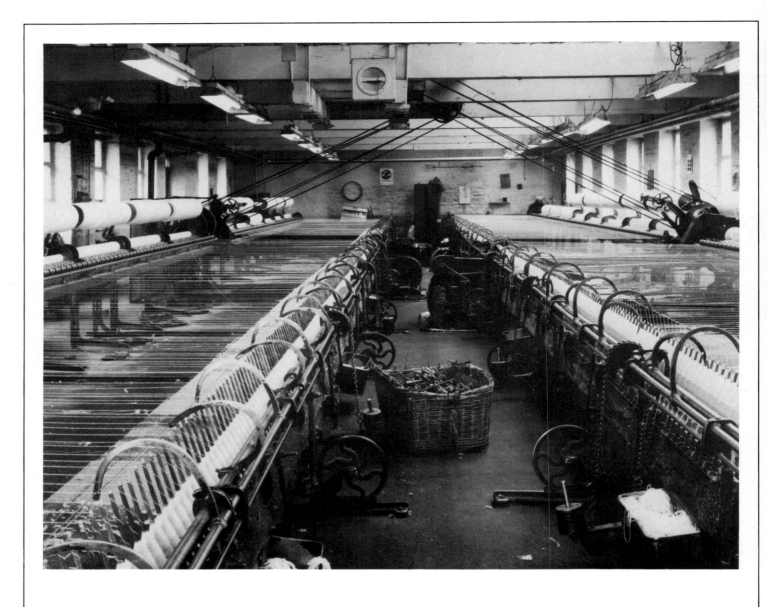

53　Mule spinning frames, Brackendale Spinning Co, Thackley, Bradford

So called because of the technological 'hybrid' invented by Samuel Crompton, a Bolton weaver, in 1780 when he combined the best features of Richard Arkwright's drawing roller with Hargreaves' spinning jenny, originally invented for cotton spinning. The mule was best suited to spinning the finer qualities of yarn and consequently taken up by the worsted side of the industry. However, in this photograph the machines are spinning woollen yarn, discernible by the tube-shaped condensers at the rear of each frame.

54   Overlooker, mule spinning, Brackendale Spinning Co
The blurred effect in this photograph is caused by the backward and forward movement of the spinning carriage.

55 Spinners, Black Dyke Mills, Queensbury

56 "Doffing", Black Dyke Mills, Queensbury
Replacing full bobbins of spun yarn for empty ones.

57 Silk spinning, Lister's Mill, Manningham

58 Doffer, Brackendale Spinning Co, Thackley, Bradford

59   Benson Turner Ltd., Wyke, Bradford
A modern plant winding and twisting acrylic fibres for knitwear.

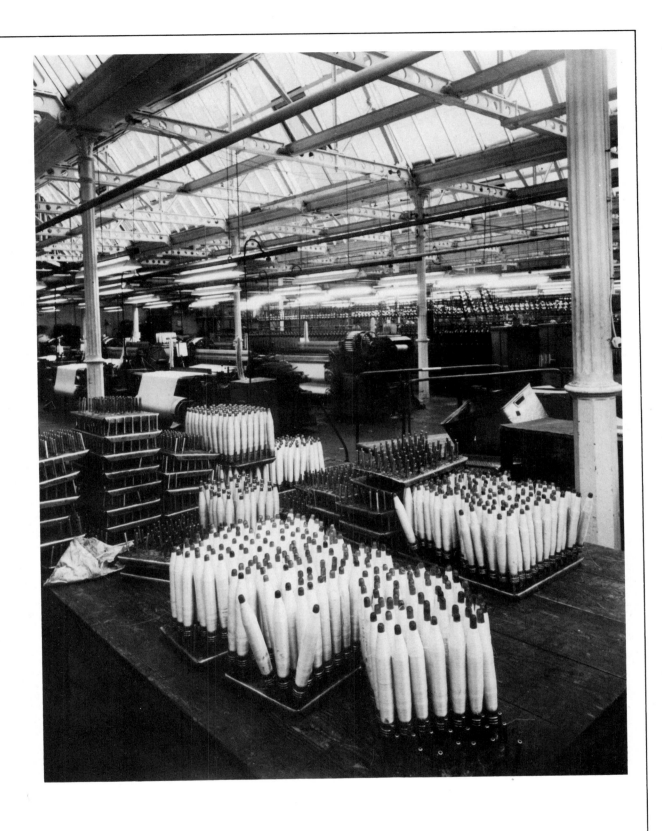

60 'Pirns', Silk Department, Lister's Mill, Bradford
The wound bobbins in the foreground are 'pirns' (packages of weft yarn which fit the shuttles of the automatic pirn-changing looms).

◀ **61 Last warping overlooker at Salts' Mill**

Here the last warping overlooker at Salts' Mill stands with some of the empty warp beams used in Sulzer looms.

▲ **62 Automatic warping at Weavercraft, Bradford**

Before the weaving process can begin the warp threads running vertically up and down the looms have to be wound tightly and side by side on to a horizontal roller called a warp beam. Each thread is passed through the eyes of the healds dependent upon the required design of the finished cloth. This was once a time consuming operation for the old handloom weaver but today's automatic warping machines have the job quickly done.

◀ **63   Weaver, Salts' Mill, Saltaire**

Those of you who bother to darn your socks will be familiar with the process of interlacing one thread (weft) under and over alternate threads (warp). This weaving process is conducted on a piece of machinery, universally known as a loom. During the 19th century, complex power looms replaced the domestic hand loom but functioned on the same basic principle of weaving. Modern Sulzer looms employ a small metal projectile much faster and quieter than the traditional shuttle. Here the weaver is repairing a broken 'end' in the warp.

▲ **64   Weaver, Pecket Well Mill, near Hebden Bridge**

65   Carpet weaving, West Yorkshire
The weaver's assistant prepares the 'creel' of a carpet loom with warp yarn.

66 'Patterns' — Salts' Mill, Saltaire

This storage unit is packed with Jacquard weaving programmes which consist of a series of punched cards for weaving complex figure patterns in the loom devised by a French silk weaver in 1801.

67 Burling and mending, Drummonds Mill, Bradford

Another stage of the finishing process is the manual skill of burling, where faults like broken ends of cloth are identified , marked and then mended, by pulling them to the back of the fabric and sewing in.

68 'Pieces', Drummonds Mill, Bradford

This is the name given to lengths of woven cloth. Here the 'grey' cloth has been woven from undyed yarn and is waiting to be dyed as a continuous length of cloth, hence it will be 'dyed in the piece'.

◀ **69 Dyehouse, Lister's Mill, Bradford**
Modern machines for dyeing the cloth in the piece.

▲ **70 Dixon's Bobbin Mills, Steeton, near Keighley**
Different spinning frames twist the fibres in different ways but they all eventually need to wind the yarn on to a wooden bobbin. Here all the paraphenalia of bobbin making clutters the workbench of a West Yorkshire bobbin makers.

◀ **71 The 'last bobbin', Dixon's Bobbin Mills, Steeton, near Keighley**
Cardboard and stiff paper tubes have come to replace traditional wooden bobbins and in January 1983 the last Yorkshire bobbin mill, at Steeton, near Keighley, closed and has subsequently been demolished.

▲ **72 Fading photographs on tool cupboard door, Dixon's Bobbin Mills, Steeton**

73 Shuttle-making, Crossleys of Todmorden ▲

The boat-shaped object carries a single thread (weft) crossways along the loom in the over and under procedure of weaving cloth. Before 1733 the weft was passed by hand across the loom limiting the width of any cloth but in that year John Kay is said to have patented his 'flying shuttle'. By tugging a cord, left and right, the wheeled shuttle (often with a pointed metal nose at each end) moved backwards and forwards across the loom. Wooden shuttles are still made today like these at Crossleys in Todmorden, but they are being superseded by metal shuttles (no bigger than a schoolboy's penknife) which can do far more picks to the minute.

74 Finished shuttles, Crossleys, Todmorden ▶

◀ **75 Foundryman's bench, Leggots Foundry, Bradford**

The wool textile industry gave rise to several secondary industries like brass and iron, founding. Here is a typical foundryman's workbench in one of West Yorkshire's numerous jobbing non-ferrous foundries. These foundries supplied valves and fittings for various machines in the wool trade. The two halves of the 'tap' mould, in the foreground, are brought together and molten brass or gun metal is poured in.

▲ **76 Treadle looms, Hattersley's of Keighley**

These looms were originally designed for weaving Harris-Tweed. Here looms await export to Third World cottage industries in 1983. Hattersley's closed shortly afterwards.

77   G. Strosse Ltd — Shoddy & Mungo Merchants, Dewsbury

The 'mungo and shoddy' trade brought much prosperity to Batley and Dewsbury and the Spen Valley for a hundred and fifty years after 1810. Shoddy is the remnants of soft woollen materials such as flannels and blankets, whereas mungo is the more superior type of woollen cloths. By mixing the two the industry can produce a thick, warm but not very durable cloth. Here this cylindrical machine armed with sharp cutting teeth is cutting woollen jackets into rags.

78   G. Strosse Ltd — Shoddy & Mungo Merchants, Dewsbury

A young woman sorts the rags in readiness for the mixing process. Rags were taken from all over the UK and formerly imported from the Continent and America.

79   G. Strosse Ltd — Shoddy & Mungo Merchants, Dewsbury

80   Sam Weller ▲

One of the few family firms to have survived the industry's upheavals in the twentieth century. Here Sam Weller like his father before him and his son of the same name stands in the office of the firm's premises in Little Germany.

81   Sam Weller's workshop ▶

The stencils in the background are for addressing bales to regular customers.

82 Wool grease extraction, Esholt Sewage Works, Bradford ▲
Scouring the wool produces a useful by-product in the form of 'lanolin' for making soaps, cosmetics, etc. The works at Bradford, apart from treating the domestic sewage, were specifically designed to extract the wool grease on a commercial basis.

83 Emptying the presses, Press House, Esholt ▶
The wool grease was extracted from the sewage by a means of steam presses.

84 'Elizabeth', Esholt Sewage Works, Bradford
This 0–4–0 saddle tank locomotive built by Hudswell Clarke (Leeds) was in service at the sewage works from 1958 until 1978. This and the sister engine 'Nelly' were both specifically designed to run on the wool grease extracted from the sewage.

85   'I'll be seeing you', Esholt Sewage Works, Bradford
*The recession of 1978–80 and the fall in the consumption of raw wool led to the closure of the Esholt sewage plant.
A redundant but optimisitc workforce looks forward to better days.*

86   Bradford from the north

Water-powered mills soon gave way to steam power and as a result textile production moved out of the countryside causing intense urbanisation of places like Huddersfield, Halifax, Dewsbury and Bradford. The size and scale of mills grew throughout the 19th century and manufacturers turned increasingly to factory production. Woollen manufacturers mechanised more gradually than their counterparts in the worsted trade.

87 Salts' New Mill

This mill was built by Titus Salt in 1868 as a spinning mill to make use of spare steam power at the works. The chimney is a copy of the campanile of the Venetian church of Santa Maria, Gloriosa.

88   Mill, Norcroft Brow, Bradford

89   Mill, Albany Street, Bradford

90 'Apply here' — Albert Mill, Bradford
A sign of better days before the Second World War when the wool textile industry was labour intensive. Technological improvements and massive rationalisation have drastically reduced the workforce.

91　Crossleys Carpet Mill, Halifax

92   Dean Clough, Halifax
The empty mills have now been redeveloped into smaller units and include an art gallery, pub, offices, studios and various manufacturing industries.

93   Mill housing, Halifax

94   View from Lister's Mill, Manningham, Bradford
The urban mills which mushroomed in West Riding towns in the nineteenth century also spawned a varying range of workpeople's cottages. These are the terraced homes of the workforce of Samuel Cunliffe Lister at Manningham almost adjacent to the weaving shed in the foreground. In the distance, Bradford's urbanisation sprawls all over Bolton and Undercliffe.

95   Main concourse, Undercliffe Cemetery, Bradford
The burial place of many merchants and mill owners.

96   Vandalised graves and lodges, Undercliffe Cemetery, Bradford
After a period of neglect the cemetery is now being restored to something of its former glory.

97 Illingworth tomb, Undercliffe Cemetery, Bradford
Perhaps the most distinctive of all the sepulchres at Undercliffe, this grey granite mausoleum in the form of an Egyptian temple marks the grave of the Illingworth family, worsted spinners of Bradford.

98   Orphans' grave at Wainstalls, near Halifax

In contrast, a simple headstone at the remote Wainstall cemetery, in the upper Calder Valley, highlights the 19th century practice of employing parish orphans whose life expectancy was considerably shortened by the harsh conditions found in mills at that time.